Making the Iron Swim

Making the Iron Swim

—⚡—

A Leadership Journey

John E. Neal

Copyright © 2019 John E. Neal

Scripture quotations marked (NLT) are taken from the Holy Bible, New Living Translation, copyright © 1996, 2004, 2015 by Tyndale House Foundation. Used by permission of Tyndale House Publishers, Inc., Carol Stream, Illinois 60188. All rights reserved.

ISBN-13: 9781091596054

"And the man of God said, 'Where fell it?' And he shewed him the place. And he cut down a stick, and cast it in thither; and the iron did swim."
(2 Kings 6:6 KJV)

Dedication

To Gwen:

Who has witnessed almost 40 years of my leadership highs and lows and still calls me her best friend.

To Abby, Grant, and Caroline:

Who have grown into incredible leaders, each in their own way. They are all a marked improvement on the original model.

Preface

I've been writing this book for almost twenty years. Not continuously, or monthly, or even sometimes for a year or two. But, the outline of this writing project never left my thoughts--and often made me feel guilty for not finishing sooner. Interestingly, over the years the tone of my writing has changed with the advancing seasons of life and work and the leadership roles that have emerged and evolved.

What began as a leadership development curriculum morphed into suggestions for being an effective leader, then culminated as reflections on the challenges of senior leadership. Now that I'm in the closing phase of my leadership journey, I'm tempted to title this book, "Recovering from the Trauma of Leadership." I could even create a local chapter of Leaders Anonymous.

"Hi, I'm John and I'm a recovering leader…"

What has emerged from decades of thinking, speaking, and writing about leadership now rests in your hands. Some of the content reflects my life and work (and successes and failures), so it may not be reflective of your experience. But, I hope you find it stimulating and helpful in your own unique journey.

The overall focus of this book is the life and work of Elisha, an Old Testament prophet presented in the Biblical passages of I Kings and II Kings. While much of the original content about Elisha was developed as chapel sermons for university students, this book was not designed as a commentary or devotional guide. Rather, I focus on Elisha as an ancient case study about being thrown into a very difficult and public role that required all of the tools of leadership to survive--including regular injections of Divine intervention.

To the extent that Elisha's example introduces or re-acquaints you with the Scriptures or with your own walk of faith, I'm happy that this study could play a small part.

Introduction

I grew up in small-town, east-central Indiana, where most people worked in automobile factories or farmed, or both. My grandfather (Mom's dad) worked second shift at our local Chrysler factory in the tool and die shop. In the years prior to elementary school (and summers thereafter), I would spend mornings with him learning practical life skills and hearing his perspectives on life.

Among his many observations was his oft-repeated quote that, "as you get older, you will have many acquaintances but few friends." In retrospect, I wish I had drilled down with him to clarify and define those two categories, but based on my own experiences, I think I can provide my own definitions, while confirming the validity of my grandfather's observations.

Friends comprise the list of people whose names could be written on the palm of your hand with a broad-tipped marker, with room to spare. You've lived life with them, including difficult times, and have come out the other side with an even stronger bond. You may not see them regularly, but when you reconnect, the days and years fall away and you pick up where you left off.

For me, acquaintances are to be enjoyed, while friends are to be cherished. One such friend is Jack. To see us together, you would think we were the original odd couple. I'm tall, he's short. I'm midwestern preppy, he's southern cowboy. I like to talk, he likes to write. Jack is my father's age, so we represent different generations, different backgrounds, different perspectives. And yet, our friendship has transcended time and distance to be a defining relationship in my life.

Both the infrequency of our communication and the mode of communication (letters and emails) would not suggest a close friendship or a tight personal bond. But Jack's appearance in print generally corresponded with significant life events (both positive and negative) that provided the key ingredients of friendship--instant reconnection, intimate communication, and seeds of encouragement that have propelled me through my life and career.

A prime example of Jack's timely notes occurred a week or so after my inauguration into my first college presidency. Jack knew from my days as a college student that I aspired some day to be the president of a small college, and so his written words from hundreds of miles away in Nashville packed more wallop than anything spoken face-to-face at the actual event (Jack would use a word like "wallop", too):

Dear John,
You'll never guess what happened this morning during a rainstorm in Guitar Gulch. Your naughty sister finally sent

me three precious items--a copy of your presidential inauguration program, a copy of your inaugural address and a copy of the newspaper with your about-to-be-hooded picture on page one.

Wow, John, what a powerful moment. Sure wish I could have been there cheering for you. I regret to inform you that at 10am on April 20, I had been captured by Klingons and forced to help one of them move who claimed to be my daughter. Believe me, I would rather have been with you than shouldering her Steinway into a truck.

I'm proud of you, John. You have grown in so many ways to become a leader in the academic community. I felt a fierce sense of pride as I read your inaugural address. Your grasp of issues, your understanding of the changing educational scene, your clear statement of goals, your ease with the common man's dreams--those elements mark you as a visionary, a president who cares, a man who loves people.

The university family welcomed you. The city fathers opened their arms to you. The political leaders and the broader academic community came to salute you. Your mom and dad could hardly contain themselves, so filled with joy and the opportunity to share this special day with you. April 20 was your day, John.

Now, it's tomorrow. Tomorrow with its unending duties and details.

Tomorrow with its high expectations and challenges. Tomorrow with its demands to make the iron swim. And you can do it all. You can handle the details. You can do your duty. You can meet the expectations. You can harness the challenges. You can make the iron swim.

I believe in you, John. I love you. I trust you. You are my friend and my brother.

An old friend,
Jack

Now, this letter may not resonate with you, but Jack's message went into my "encouragement" file (also Jack's idea), where I keep my special letters and notes. I pull these rays of sunshine out of my file whenever the days are dark and my spirits are sagging. Over the years, I have reread the phrase "make the iron swim" a hundred times, remembering with each reading its reference to the Old Testament prophet Elisha and his miraculous levitation of metal in the river.

Several months later, I was approached on campus by a student ministry group looking for a new approach to weekly chapel services. They proposed a study on leadership focusing on the life lessons of a Bible character. Remembering Jack's reference, I began a deeper examination of Elisha's life and leadership, and this book was conceived. The concepts that follow are mine, but the inspiration was pure Jack.

Jack inspired the concept of this book at what I considered to be the pinnacle of my career--a too-ambitious, much-too-young

Making the Iron Swim

academic leader ascending to a college presidency when most young adults are still trying to decide on a career track. The concepts that follow, however, were developed and refined over a couple of decades of lectures, seminars, retreats and discussions. In Elisha, we find the essence of a successful leader--born in obscurity, called to follow a mercurial and inconsistent mentor, faithfully fulfilling his calling throughout a long and demanding career (and in spite of some notable missteps), and continuing to influence the lives of others long after his death. I hope the insights provided by Elisha encourage you in your leadership journey--and may you always "make the iron swim".

I
The Call of Leadership

Stroll down the aisle of any bookstore, and you will find an absolute cacophony of titles on leadership:

"How I Became a Leader in 5 Easy Steps"
"Win, Win, Win"
"See it, Grab it"
"Jiminy Cricket on Leadership"

OK, I made up the titles (I hope), but you get the idea. While a number of excellent books on leadership grace my own office bookshelves, a growing number of titles advance notions of leadership based on power, position, influence, and prestige.

Ironically, while the focus on leadership continues to expand and increase, the stated need for effective leaders also continues to grow within our organizations. It would be too obvious a sales ploy for me to denigrate the available literature for aspiring leaders while promoting my own "breakthrough" for dynamic leadership.

John E. Neal

Unfortunately, I bring no profound words of wisdom, no original pearls of insight to offer as an example of extraordinary leadership. But, as a seasoned, often struggling, too-frequently flawed leader, I am constantly looking for helpful examples to study and emulate. In Elisha's life story, we see a balanced, real-world case study of sustained and effective leadership that lasted a lifetime and beyond.

In sum, Elisha's life provides a number of key insights that align with the characteristics of true leaders:

1) Leaders are neither born nor made--they are *willing*.
As the eternal debate rages regarding the characteristics of a great leader (natural ability versus cultivated skills), Elisha mirrors the typical scenario for the newly enlisted leader--a willingness to step away from the familiar into the frightening realm of the unknown, and usually in much too public a setting. Elisha's narrative offers little information about his background and circumstances. Why did Elijah tap Elisha on the shoulder? Plowing with a team of oxen hardly displayed the classic traits of a potential prophet/leader--although most leaders will equate leading groups of people with herding various types of animals (including the danger of where to next step). What we do know from this narrative is Elisha's willingness to leave the familiar and accept a new path of life and leadership.

Many leaders I know echo the same theme, especially in academic circles. No master plan, no detailed scheming. Someone, somewhere, with a tap on the shoulder and a question, request, or challenge to take a step out of the furrow they were plowing into a different field of endeavor. From anonymity to visibility. From routine to unpredictable. From plowing with oxen to leading the spiritual direction of a nation.

Our lives may not reach the astounding dimensions of Elisha's, but our leadership journeys often begin in much the same way. The gentle tap on the shoulder (or phone call or email) with an unassuming inquiry beginning with, "have you ever thought about," or "we need someone to take charge of this project." Simple, small steps that slowly ease us out of our familiar current path and shift our point of reference on the horizon to something unimagined.

Leonard Sweet[1] summarizes the concept well in his book *Summoned to Lead*:

> *"To put it bluntly: the whole leadership thing is a demented concept. Leaders are neither born nor made. Leaders are summoned. They are called into existence by circumstances. Those who rise to the occasion are leaders."*

2) Leaders rarely follow a predictable path of leadership development; most experience alternating phases of the mundane and the miraculous (and must survive both)

Elisha's story of the floating axehead inspired the title of this book and serves as the ideal example of the typical leader's life. Chopping wood one minute and making iron swim the next. A friend of mine who just retired after a career in the army says that the life of an officer is long periods of boredom punctuated by

---

[1] Leonard Sweet (2009) *Summoned to Lead*. Grand Rapids: Zondervan.

short bursts of terror. Not only can leadership be less than glamorous, it can be downright tedious and boring.

As difficult as the mundane and demeaning aspects of leadership may be, the challenges of surviving our own success may be even greater. Elisha's flashes of ego--communicated through attitude, word, and action--remind us of our own tendencies to believe our own PR, and to take ourselves too seriously. We are tempted to take more credit for the success of our organization than we deserve, and most deadly, to grow accustomed to the trappings often associated with leadership--power, prestige, and position. Elisha illustrates through his life, and through his own open disregard for people in powerful positions, that we aren't as brilliant, or funny, or all-powerful as we think we have become.

3) The keys to successful leadership are preparation and persistence

Whenever I speak to groups about leadership, inevitably I'll observe two distinct reactions--those engaged and energized by the topic, and those who sit back and shut down. I used to believe that the study of leadership was one of life's dichotomies, where everyone in the world either loves it or hates it (like eating coconut or watching Star Wars or listening to Barry Manilow). But, the development of leadership isn't merely a preference or option or hobby for most of us. Once we're willing to lead, we quickly see the necessity of developing key capacities and skills.

I love cycling (that's bicycling, not motorcycling). I'm embarrassed to tell you that I ride a $3,000 bike. The cyclists reading this are thinking, "wow, that's a cheap bike," while you non-cyclists are wondering if my wife makes me sleep in the garage with my bike. But, I understand that my passion and commitment to riding isn't shared by many of my friends (including my wife), but that's ok. Everyone doesn't have to ride along.

But, a lack of natural affinity for the study of leadership doesn't excuse current and future leaders from their responsibility to nurture and develop the skill sets that will serve their teams and organizations well. Underperforming organizations are rife with underprepared leaders who didn't have the interest, drive, or passion to prepare for their leadership opportunities, while many seasoned leaders often plateau in their personal and professional growth due to a lack of interest or energy--and their organizations plateau as well.

In an era of leadership bravado and braggadocio--regardless of the organizational setting--the tendency of seasoned leaders to adopt a "been there, done that, trust me" mentality creates the likelihood of major disaster as rapidly changing external and internal forces encounter entrenched (and arrogant) leaders. Each one separately is difficult to manage. Together, they are deadly for any leader and anyone around them. Elisha provides ample lessons on adaptability and shifting approaches to fit the audience and the context.

Which brings us back to our study of Elisha as a leader and the key factors that emerge from his example:

- **A Clear Call to Lead**--Elisha encountered a distinct call to step away from his current circumstances and to pursue a new direction. The choice was his to make and he chose the more challenging path.

- **Consistency Over Many Years**--In spite of his apprenticeship with an inconsistent and moody mentor (Elijah), Elisha maintains a remarkable consistency of purpose, drive, and character throughout his life.
- **Prophet as Leader vs. Prophet as Ascetic**--Prophets occupied an unusual position in ancient times. As an intermediary between God and His people, prophets often found the meditative life in communion with God more soothing and fulfilling that dealing with living, breathing, frustrating human beings. Elisha maintains close fellowship with God, but brings the fruit of that relationship out to the everyday lives of people, while also living a public life as an example to others.
- **An Extensive and Public Record**--Unlike some other Biblical characters, Elisha provides a wide variety of materials to examine, representing various contexts and challenges for leadership, as well as the challenges of leading over a long period of time.

I hope this study will expand your capacity for internal awareness and growth, as you also cultivate community with other aspirational leaders and identify specific actions to enhance your leadership effectiveness.

Part 1
Starting Well

"If God has given you leadership ability, take the responsibility seriously."

—Romans 12:8 (NLT)

11
Start with the End in Sight

> *"Then Elisha died and was buried. Groups of Moabite raiders used to invade the land each spring. Once when some Israelites were burying a man, they spied a band of these raiders. So they hastily threw the corpse into the tomb of Elisha and fled. But as soon as the body touched Elisha's bones, the dead man revived and jumped to his feet!"*

—2 Kings 13:20-21 (NLT)

I'm one of those people who sneaks a peek at the end of a book to see how it ends, long before I'm finished reading it. It isn't that I want to spoil the ending. I've found that knowing the ending in advance can often sharpen my reading skills to identify and connect seemingly unrelated events in the story that build to the ultimate climax and resolution. Starting with the end in mind helps me focus on the essential elements of the plot while ignoring the superfluous and unnecessary distraction crafted by the author.

It's a skill I've tried to develop in my life and leadership as well, sometimes successfully and sometimes--to my own detriment--not well at all. Through both positive and negative reinforcement, I've learned that keeping the end in sight provides clarity and focus as we encounter myriad distractions in our lives and in our leadership opportunities. And so it is with Elisha. We begin with his final story--as a corpse in a cave--to illustrate the ultimate leadership legacy.

My maternal grandmother, Granny, lived to be 97 years old. My last time with her was during a New Year's trip home. Sitting with her on my parents' couch, she asked, "Why has God left me here so long?" I reminded her that before Jesus left the earth he said he was going to prepare a place for us. "I guess he's not finished with your place, yet, Granny. It must be some place to see."

A few months later, Granny's five grandchildren, all grown with children of their own, gathered to speak at her funeral. All five told vastly different stories illustrating her love and devotion and impact in their lives. Yet all five grandchildren ended their talk with the same underlying theme--that Granny loved them more than the other four!

More than the grilled bologna sandwiches, the homemade egg noodles, or the sacrificial financial investment she made for each of us (paying for all five to attend college out of her meager savings account), we all remembered her ability to make us feel like the center of her universe.

When my turn came to speak, I learned two important lessons. One, I can weep and speak at the same time, and two, all

Making the Iron Swim

of the faces looking up at me from the front rows of that little church shared a strong familial resemblance to Granny. Not only was her physical DNA replicated in all of us, but her loving leadership was reflected in all of us--and now through us, and into the lives of countless others.

She really did love me best, by the way.

Elisha's story of the corpse in the cave provides two important goals for any aspirational leader:

1) Building a Good Name

> *"Choose a good reputation over great riches; being held in high esteem is better than silver or gold."*
>
> —Proverbs 22:1 (NLT)

I've been a "pleaser" all my life, which means that I have a constant need for people to like me, to appreciate the work that I do. Of course, it also makes me insatiable for pats on the back and words of praise. I think it's a reason why I started my adult life as a musician. The feedback was immediate and public, and nothing compares to enthusiastic applause from an audience. However, as a leader, I've discovered that receiving praise from colleagues and friends is not the same as building a good name.

We fall into this trap regularly, of confusing what we do and achieve with who we are as a person and leader. We point to our accomplishments, to our level of sustained productivity, and forget to attend to the underlying content of our lives and the conduct of our character--which ultimately becomes the fabric of our long-term reputation and our good name.

A good name, our reputation as leaders, takes a lifetime to build, but a moment to destroy. Long after our accomplishments have been forgotten and new leaders take our place, people will remember how our decisions helped to build or tarnish our good name. Elisha's tomb was distinguished by the person it contained.

2) Making a Sustained Impact

I've been fortunate to work in two very different worlds--education technology start-ups, and higher education. Generalizations about either world are not completely accurate nor fair, but I have found archetypes of people within each that promote personal agendas at the expense of leadership legacies, both for the person leading and for those within their sphere of influence.

The venture capital world is not the den of thieves that popular culture would lead us to believe, but I have lots of experience with early and mid-career executives who view their current position as little more than a stepping stone to the next big opportunity (which ultimately leads to the big chair and the even bigger financial payoff they envision). I equate this leadership phenomenon to the person at dinner who is sitting with you but scanning the room for someone more important or attractive. Even if the organization advances and succeeds in the short run, the continual grasping and elbowing and stepping over other people to advance one's career creates an abiding cynicism about leaders (or executives) in general, and minimizes a leader's long-term impact within that organization, or over a lifetime.

Within the academy (that's what we academics call university life), the opposite is often true. Attend any gathering of new college presidents, provosts, or deans, and you will hear lots of protestations about how the mantle was cast upon their shoulders, much to their chagrin and regret. The old adage of "those who can, do, and those who can't, teach" is often extended by faculty as "and those who can't teach become administrators." I remember a visit from a mid-career professor to my office early in my first college presidency. After a brief discussion of our topic of business, he slowly took a 360 degree scan of my office and said, "yeah, I could've done this...if I had wanted to!"

Whether or not an administrative role is a step down for an academic, the reality remains that many people in an organization don't aspire to lead, nor do they want to divert their attention and energies from the career track they envisioned when they began their formal schooling or their early job choices. Unfortunately, a cultural disdain for leadership, or a minimizing of the importance of leadership in the life of organizations, can discourage the aspirations of early and mid-career members of a team who have considered taking the step, or have been asked to move outside their comfort zone.

Certainly, our legacies will not extend in the same way as Elisha's--bringing the dead back to life after making contact with our bones! But, as we attend to the factors that build a good name and make a sustained impact--in other words, as we start our leadership journey with the end in sight--we breathe life and vitality into the lives of those around us, especially after our functional leadership days are finished.

III

A Tap on the Shoulder

"So Elijah went and found Elisha son of Shophat plowing a field with a team of oxen. There were eleven teams of oxen ahead of his, and he was plowing with the twelfth team. Elijah went over to him and threw his cloak across his shoulders and walked away again.

Elisha left the oxen standing there, ran after Elijah, and said to him, 'First let me go and kiss my father and mother good-bye, and then I will go with you!' Elijah replied, 'Go back! But consider what I have done to you.'

Elisha then returned to his oxen, killed them, and used the wood from the plow to build a fire to roast their flesh. He passed around the meat to the other plowmen, and they all ate. The he went with Elijah as his assistant."

—1 Kings 19:19-21 (NLT)

Po Bronson in his sociological study of life and work entitled, *What Should I Do With My Life*[2], concludes that the single greatest drive today is finding our role in life:

"We are all writing the story of our life. We want to know what it's 'about', what are its themes and which theme is on the rise. We demand of it something deeper, or richer, or more substantive. We want to know where we're headed--not to spoil our own ending by ruining the surprise, but we want to ensure that when the ending comes, it won't be shallow. We will have done something. We will not have squandered our time here."

Whatever our vocational choices, we all face the inevitable opportunities to move from spectator to participant in the realm of leadership--reminding us again of our need to respond to the question "are you willing?"

Steven Sample in his book, *Contrarian's Guide to Leadership*[3] calls us to "do leadership." As we move from thinking about

---

[2] Po Bronson (2003) *What Should I Do With My Life?* New York: Random House.
[3] Steven B. Sample (2002) *The Contrarian's Guide to Leadership.* San Francisco: Jossey-Bass.

leadership to action, how do we start? And, more importantly, how do we start well? In this passage from 1 Kings 19, Elijah challenges Elisha to "consider" what Elijah had proposed and the implications of the decision to pursue a path of leadership. In the same way, emerging leaders need to preface their leadership journey with three basic considerations:

1) **What does a leader do? (Definition)**
2) **How do I know I'm called to lead? (Clarification)**
3) **Will I be a good leader? (Evaluation)**

Defining Leadership

Whenever I'm teaching a course or seminar on leadership, I'll ask the participants to compile a brief list of the most effective leaders they have known personally. I'm always amazed that by adding the "personal" dimension, the students change their focus from leadership of mythical proportions (Martin Luther King, Jr.; Mahatma Gandhi; John F. Kennedy) to leaders at the grassroots, practical level.

I follow the listing exercise with the question, "What characteristics do these effective leaders display?" The memory of those influential leaders results in a very different kind of list than they may have originally associated with high-impact leaders. Rather than compiling a theoretical and grandiose list of textbook characteristics of leadership--what I refer to as the "Superman Syndrome of Leadership" (able to leap tall buildings, faster than a speeding bullet, more powerful than a locomotive)--the resulting lists focus on the impact of leaders on their own lives. The

Making the Iron Swim

"doing" of leadership then appears (empowers, inspires, challenges, demonstrates).

Elisha witnessed a powerful leader in Elijah, but observation alone is insufficient to build an effective leader. As an educator, I've witnessed the transition of teaching from being "the sage on the stage" to serving as a guide and facilitator of learning. It's tough to stop talking and focus more on the student, but all the empirical evidence on learning shows that students learn more when they are actively involved in the process. But, it's easy to say and hard to do.

Maybe that's why we're regularly frustrated with critical processes in our lives. They often fall short of our expectations and our needs, whether it's new employee orientation, college degrees, discipleship programs, or getting our kids to pick up their stuff. We're spending most of our time telling and little time showing. So, our organizations suffer from a dearth of "leaders under development", because we don't have the time, inclination, or ability to move our processes beyond the superficial and pre-packaged. What do we DO about this? What are the essential ingredients in helping aspiring or called leaders to develop skills, insights, and attitudes conducive to effective leadership?

New Leaders Require Parenting, Not Just Reproduction (Clarification)

Much of the existing literature on leadership highlights the necessity of *reproduction,* that is, leaders begat leaders. Whatever the particular field of endeavor, great leaders assemble a cadre of "heirs apparent", while these handpicked, emerging leaders carry

John E. Neal

the imprimatur of the master leader into their next phase of life and work.

But, the notion of reproduction only skims the surface of the deeper workings necessary for developing leadership capacity. That richer dimension more closely resembles *parenting* than merely *birthing* a new generation.

Several months ago, my wife and I resigned our work responsibilities in Chicago and moved to Nashville so that we could assist our extended family in caring for my parents. For my mom, the challenges involved some memory and cognition issues, but for my dad (whom I've always called Pop), it was strictly (and profoundly) physical. In fact, so clear was his mind, that several days after lapsing into an extended coma, Pop opened his eyes, asked that day's date, and asked my mother, "did you write the rent check?"

That clarity of thought allowed us to enjoy a season of parenting I'm still processing. Upon my return to Nashville, I began to appreciate the incredible dynamic of four generations of Neal boys (Pop, me, my son, and my grandson). All four the sole male of their generation--the last of the family line for each era.

For each of us, that interconnectedness illustrated and reinforced the changing roles and needs we represented within the family tree. Pop realized his remaining days were short, yet he gained strength and energy from long discussions about people, places and events from 80+ years of living. Pop was always a big storyteller, so his facile mind was a gift that gave him purpose and meaning when all the other parts of his body failed him.

I found that my professional transition from structured work to consulting permitted a level of flexibility that allowed longer unstructured sessions with Pop. Our conversations often involved a recapping of a current project or a debriefing of a conversation. These interactions gave Pop a sense of connection to my world, while providing me with a safe harbor for talking through challenging consulting issues. Most of all, my months with Pop allowed me to slow down, to be more reflective in my work, and to be more selective in how I wanted to invest my time, especially when other--more valuable--experiences were available. Today, I find that my work satisfaction comes from engaging in interesting projects that connect me with good people, and not just being busy for the sake of busyness.

And now, right in front of me, my son is making the transition to being an adult--carrying the mantle of responsibility for a family while feeling the satisfaction of a career direction that finds traction and momentum. I'm slowly incorporating into our conversation the lessons I've learned these past months from Pop, especially the provision of a warm, supportive haven for my son's recounting of daily challenges and opportunities.

I'm also thoroughly enjoying the chance to watch my son develop his own unique parenting techniques, as he guides my grandson in building the basic tools for life--how to behave, how to speak to others, how to hit a baseball (and understanding that sometimes you strike out).

Making the Grade (Evaluation)

We want to grow and develop as leaders, but we avoid--or chafe--at efforts to assess our leadership or evaluate our effectiveness. In human resources terminology, we often are the focus of summative evaluation, but rarely receive formative assessment.

Broadly defined, summative evaluation takes place at defined intervals, such as an annual review, and seeks to score attitudes, actions and results in light of organizational themes and specific individual goals. Typically, summative evaluation serves one of two purposes: 1) to reassure the employee that expectations are being met--with the financial rewards associated with the overall score or rating, or 2) to motivate the employee to begin moving in a new direction, whether upward in productivity or out the door.

Unfortunately, much of the summative evaluation performed in our organizations is short-lived and tied to immediate rewards. Much like the "teaching to the test" happening in some schools looking to vault standardized test scores at the expense of longer-term intellectual achievement, we focus our leadership development processes on those attributes most easily observed and measured, and the outcomes that advance our short-term financial and organizational goals.

Formative evaluation expands the leadership development conversation to broader themes, attributes and characteristics that will assess the leader--and the organization--across longer time horizons and beyond the demands of the immediate or expedient. But, formative assessment brings its own challenges. Effective formative review requires the development of trust between the participants and the investment of significant time--both precious commodities for any aspiring or seasoned leader. Even CEOs find themselves torn between wanting candid feedback and needing to guard against any admission of shortcoming or failure--whether personal or professional.

Whether in for-profit or not-for-profit organizations, CEOs receive the bulk of their evaluation and assessment from an executive committee, usually a subset of the board of directors. Typically, the annual review focuses on achievement of strategic benchmarks, as identified through key performance metrics. Continued employment and incentive compensation (which constitutes the majority of CEOs pay structure these days) permeates every question and topic of discussion.

At some point at the end of the review, the "softer" side of the assessment appears, usually following this script:

"So, how are you...really?"
Followed by this response by the CEO:
"I'm fine...really."

After a number of other soft probes into the general wellbeing of the CEO (including some bromides about not burning out and spending time with family), the conversation concludes with:

"Anything you'd like to share?"
To which the CEO responds:
"No, I'm good...really."

Consequently, those holding the power of employment rarely hear transparency and candor from leaders, especially about personal faults and failures, until the hidden issues become public problems. To transition the leadership development conversation beyond evaluation to sustained formation, our structures and systems must expand from the summative goals of evaluation (motive, reward, rank among peers) to a relationship built on trust, transparency, and a commitment of time that permits the sculpting of leadership potential into reality for our organizations.

IV
Pass the Torch

"So Elijah went and found Elisha son of Shophat plowing a field with a team of oxen. There were eleven teams of oxen ahead of his, and he was plowing with the twelfth team. Elijah went over to him and threw his cloak across his shoulders and walked away again.

Elisha left the oxen standing there, ran after Elijah, and said to him, 'First let me go and kiss my father and mother good-bye, and then I will go with you!' Elijah replied, 'Go back! But consider what I have done to you.'

Elisha then returned to his oxen, killed them, and used the wood from the plow to build a fire to roast their flesh. He passed around the meat to the other

> *plowmen, and they all ate. Then he went with Elijah as his assistant."*

—1 Kings 19:19-21 (NLT)

No, you're not experiencing deja vu. I did list the same passage from 1 Kings as in Chapter Three. But, rather than viewing the exchange from Elisha's perspective--and his critical decision about becoming a leader--re-read the passage from Elijah's side of the exchange:

"So Elijah went and found Elisha..." Where had Elijah been? On Mount Sinai, the mountain of God. But, in a cave being fed by an angel of the Lord after fleeing for his life from Jezebel. In business circles, you meet people who have the entrepreneurial spirit, sometimes coupled with a high tolerance for risk, who make and lose multiple fortunes in their lives. Elijah follows a similar pattern in his spiritual leadership. Call fire from heaven, followed by praying for death alone under a broom tree, leading to a personal encounter with God, so that Elijah can whine about doing all the work all by himself. God's solution? Get some help.

"...plowing a field with a team of oxen." Lewis Grizzard[4] said, "If you ain't the lead dog, the scenery never changes." Elisha was plowing with the last team of oxen. Twelfth of twelve. The scenery wasn't changing. Elijah wisely perceived Elisha to be an under-utilized resource. But, it's scary to leave what we know, even if it's not comfortable or pleasant. Sometimes it's easier to

---

[4] Lewis Grizzard (1994) *The Wit and Wisdom of Lewis Grizzard*. Atlanta: Longstreet Press.

complain about current circumstances than to take a step into the unknown.

"Elijah...threw his cloak across his (Elisha's) shoulders..." A public sign of succession. Not an instantaneous transition, but the beginning of instruction. Great leaders constantly identify and instruct new leaders, either for their current role or for other leadership positions. Additionally, thoughtful leaders help their successors transition seamlessly to maintain momentum. Egotistical leaders think, "everything will fall apart when I leave, which will show how indispensible I am."

"...consider what I have done to you." Leadership transitions are never blind leaps of faith. Informed choice--careful calculation--plays as critical a role in the transition as personal courage and professional curiosity.

"Elisha then returned to his oxen, killed them, and used the wood from the plow to build a fire to roast their flesh." Perhaps not as dramatic as the story of Cortez burning his ships upon landing in Mexico in 1519, but Elisha provides a visible commitment to his leadership calling.

"Then he (Elisha) went with Elijah as his assistant." In today's jargon, Elijah and Elisha began a mentoring relationship. But, what constitutes mentoring versus simply spending time together or sharing insights between a seasoned leader and an aspiring one?

The Mentoring Process

Certainly, the mentoring relationship involves a significant amount of *instruction*. Too often, the content of that instruction focuses either on the mentor's area of expertise or the student's comfort zone. Anyone who has worked with me will tell you that I love focusing on strategy and creating new initiatives, which also involves negotiating with external parties. One CEO with whom I served once referred to me as the "director of new stuff." No one has to motivate me to work in these spheres. I gravitate there and find my greatest fulfillment in those kinds of activities.

On the other hand, I have to drag myself into operational issues. Making the machinery hum. Keeping the trains arriving on time. It's important, essential, and complex work, and I ignore it at my own (and the organization's) peril. But, it isn't my natural inclination. So, when I'm mentoring someone for senior leadership, I point them to the very best operational people I know, who share the secrets of effective and efficient operations.

The student also brings natural gifts and abilities to the mentoring relationship, which raises the challenge of how to spend instructional time for highest impact. In baseball terms, do we focus on making a pitcher the best pitcher possible, or on building other skill sets (hitting, for instance) to balance the player's contributions? As leaders, we have an obligation to understand and contribute to conversations across the organization, but does the mentoring relationship aim for equal balance in all things or excellence in some things, with adequacy in others? I don't have definite answers, but these topics provide a helpful context at the beginning of any mentoring discussion.

Mentoring also provides an opportunity for ***observation***, providing context for leadership decisions and challenges. The application of what we know about leading through the practice of leadership opens doors of discussion about wisdom as a leader-—knowing what to do, when to do it, and how to implement it effectively. As with the content dilemma, mentors should open doors of observation with other seasoned leaders who excel in areas not found in the mentor's skill set.

Early in my doctoral studies in higher education leadership, I was required to take a course in finance, for which I had little or no background (did I mention I started out as a musician?). At the time, I had just been awarded a research assistantship, which required me to work with a seasoned researcher and for which I received both a scholarship and a stipend. A divine miracle for a starving graduate student who was married with two children. My finance professor was leading a discussion on "extramural funding", which is a fancy term for grants. Of course, I had nothing to add to the discussion, being the newbie to the field. My professor exclaimed,

"Neal, you work within a grant award, you're paid by the grant, and you get a scholarship from the grant. But you know nothing about grants?"

"Right."

"Well, then I'm making an appointment for you to meet the university's chief grant officer."

"Yay…"

It turns out that the introduction intended to be remedial was transformational. I don't know why he did it, but Steve, a highly regarded grants executive at a major research university, turned a brief introductory conversation into an opportunity for me to observe leadership first-hand. Rather than turning me into another unpaid intern who picks up coffee and runs the copy machine, Steve allowed me to attend meetings, observe his interactions with key individuals and constituencies, and provided extended moments of debriefing and instruction.

While my introduction to grants administration was interesting and helpful, the deeper lessons I learned from Steve through observation provided foundational concepts for my future mentoring and leadership:

Embrace the fear inherent in change. My doctoral studies in higher education were a dramatic shift from two degrees and several years of experience in music. From my first class, I realized that my lack of previous coursework and professional experience in the field put me at a marked disadvantage among my peers. During my initial meeting with Steve, the fear and intimidation came rushing out. When Steve asked my background, I said "I'm a musician trying to make the shift to higher education." When I asked Steve his background, he replied, "I'm a musician with two degrees in music and a doctorate in higher education." Hmmm. So, perhaps my finance professor wasn't punishing me by sending me to Steve. Steve had made the transition and successfully. The relief was palpable.

You don't have to know everything--and you shouldn't act like you do. Steve is one of the top experts in the country regarding research and grants administration, which is the result of decades of work in a specific area of responsibility. But, there are also areas within university work for which he has little or no knowledge or experience. In academic circles, we often view having a PhD as being an expert. About everything. Then we wonder why people view us with suspicion, or even disdain. Steve would tell me when he was confident about a topic, when he had an opinion on a subject, and when he had a person he wanted me to meet to learn about a subject.

Quiet, calm, and kindness are critical learned behaviors. As my first mentor in higher education leadership, Steve modeled three critical personal traits: 1) In musical terms, Steve always spoke at a *mezzo piano*, and never raised his voice in my presence...ever; 2) working in the grants field puts you in the middle of arguments about money regularly--who has it, who gets it, who controls it--yet Steve was an oasis of calm in the midst of frequent faculty storms; and 3) academe by its very nature is status conscious and power hungry, especially at the "elite" universities, and everyone thinks they are elite. Steve embodied a kind spirit and exuded that kindness to everyone, whether they were being kind or not in return.

I wish I could say that Steve's leadership concepts found fallow ground in my own personality and bore much fruit. Truth be told, I'm amazed at how quickly the lessons learned were sidelined by my own notions of "leadership." Never admitting what I didn't know, for fear of being seen as dumb or weak. Driving hard, fast, and furiously to achieve things that would further propel my reputation and career. I'm reminded of a conversation with an early supervisor at my first university after graduate school.

Over lunch, my boss said,

"John, you are the most ambitious person I've ever met."

"Thanks!"

"That was not a compliment..."

But, I've come to realize that mentoring builds on the long view, not a short glance. In pedagogical terms, effective mentors have a

John E. Neal

specific outcome in mind--***Wisdom***. The *Cambridge Dictionary*[5] defines "wisdom" as "the ability to make good judgments based on what you have learned from your experience." So, instruction combined with observation builds a basis for the development of good judgment, sprinkled liberally with ***encouragement*** and driven by a persistent ***commitment*** to the development of a leader.

---

5 *Cambridge School Dictionary* (2008) Cambridge: Cambridge University Press.

V
Be Persistent

"When the LORD was about to take Elijah up to heaven in a whirlwind, Elijah and Elisha were traveling from Gilgal. And Elijah said to Elisha, 'Stay here, for the LORD has told me to go to Bethel.' But Elisha replied, 'As surely as the LORD lives and you yourself live, I will never leave you!' So they went down together to Bethel....

Then Elijah said to Elisha, 'Stay here, for the LORD has told me to go to Jericho.' But Elisha replied again, 'As surely as the LORD lives and you yourself live, I will never leave you.' So they went together to Jericho....

Then Elijah said to Elisha, 'Stay here, for the LORD has told me to go to the Jordan River.' But again Elisha replied, 'As surely as the LORD lives and you yourself live, I will never leave you.' So they went on together. Fifty men from the group of prophets also went and watched from a distance as Elijah and Elisha stopped beside the Jordan River. Then Elijah folded his cloak together and struck the water with it. The river divided, and the two of them went across on dry ground!

When they came to the other side, Elijah said to Elisha, 'Tell me what I can do for you before I am taken away.' And Elisha replied, 'Please let me inherit a double share of your spirit and become your successor.' 'You have asked a difficult thing,' Elijah replied. 'If you see me when I am taken from you, then you will get your request. But if not, then you won't.'

As they were walking along and talking, suddenly a chariot of fire appeared, drawn by horses of fire. It drove between the two men, separating them, and Elijah was carried by a whirlwind into heaven. Elisha saw it and cried out, 'My father! My father! I see the chariots and charioteers of Israel!' And as they disappeared from sight, Elisha tore his clothes in distress.

Elisha picked up Elijah's cloak, which had fallen when he was taken up. Then Elisha returned

Making the Iron Swim

to the bank of the Jordan River. He struck the water with Elijah's cloak and cried out, 'Where is the LORD, the God of Elijah?' Then the river divided, and Elisha went across."

—2 KINGS 2:1-2; 4; 6-14 (NLT)

I grew up a small child on a small street in a small town in central Indiana populated by big kids. Not only was I the youngest in the large, roving group of teens and pre-teens in the neighborhood, I was literally the smallest kid among the boys. The main leaders in the neighborhood measured 6'11", 6'9", 6'7", and 6'5". And then there was me, the runt. Fortunately, my sister was bigger than me, and willing to fight battles for her little brother. Which I was more than happy to let her do, since it distracted her from beating up on me.

As the neighborhood runt, I was the annoying shadow to every game, every conversation, every adventure. The phrase I recall most often from my childhood? "Get lost!" In a basketball-crazed state, I lived in the most basketball-crazed town of 20,000 people, who built a fieldhouse that seated 10,000 people and filled it regularly. So, my father attached a basketball goal to the garage behind our house, where his runt son could sit and watch the big boys shoot hoops for hours on end. And occasionally get in a shot or two.

That's where I learned the art of persistence. To keep taking shots even when most of them get blocked back into your face. To alter moves and approaches to get an open shot. To adjust the trajectory of your shot to avoid the high jumps and long arms. In fifth grade, I was selected for my first real team in a city league. The head coach who selected me said, "John, you play pretty well, but your shot has too high of an arch." To which I replied, "You don't play at my house…if it doesn't go up, it'll never go in."

Those lessons on the driveway of my childhood home helped me through years of being incredibly average as a basketball player, but also in managing other situations where I wasn't the biggest, smartest, or most gifted person. In the passage above, Elisha displays incredible persistence, even when Elijah seems determined to tell him to "get lost!" But, Elijah wisely interprets Elisha's persistence as a key ingredient to his future success as a leader.

Elijah couldn't shake him. This passage from 2 Kings records three times that Elijah says "stay" and Elisha says "no." I don't know if there were other occasions or just these three, but they were sufficient to wear Elijah down. As a leader, I must listen for and reward persistence in my staff members, and not just communicate "get lost", no matter how subtle or sophisticated the message.

Elijah couldn't fool him. While Elijah didn't lie to Elisha, he certainly implied that God told Elijah to go and Elisha to stay. But, Elisha wasn't buying it. I'm reminded of my interactions with my children and now my grandchildren. The myriad activities that the child could repeat endlessly, but you're sick and tired of doing. Or you have something more important to do, like sitting down and putting your feet up. So, you make an excuse, being careful to be truthful without hurting their feelings. But, they don't buy it. They want to come along and be a part of what you're doing. And exhaustion leads to relenting, to giving into the boundless energy that says "I love you, I respect you, and I want to experience what you're experiencing in this moment."

Persistence displays commitment. Elisha's persistence expressed the inexpressible--that he would do anything and go anywhere to be with Elijah. As leaders who mentor and students who follow, persistence opens doors to investments in learning that help grow both partners in the mentoring relationship.

As a *student*, our persistence reveals itself through:

- **Willingness to learn**

University students (and parents and employers and government agencies) often confuse getting a degree with actual learning. In this consumer-driven era of higher education, faculty members and deans often hear students say, "just tell me what I need to do to get my course credit and my degree." In fact, now that the largest segment of higher education enrollments are of non-traditional age, some adult students regularly say to professors, "I've been working in this field for years, and I know more about it than you do." As if there is nothing left to learn, no room left to grow.

- **Submission to authority**

As a child of the '60s, I have witnessed a societal shift in attitudes toward leaders from unmerited reverence to unnecessary antagonism. As a college professor and administrator, I have never expected my students to kiss my feet, although I have been tempted once or twice to tell someone to do just that in the heat of an argument. But, conversely, I continue to be shocked by the open disdain I feel from students of all ages who question the integrity, intelligence, or humanity of any leader who dares correct their work, highlights weaknesses in their academic submissions, or simply tells them that they can't "have it their way".

In recent years, a popular concept in Christian circles has been the notion that true disciples become covered with the dust of their rabbi's sandals. Whether or not the concept is historically accurate, the word picture helps illuminate the proper balance of submission. Not subservient nor blindly obedient, but thoughtfully observing the trail blazed by the master teacher and mentor.

- **Reflection of the mentor**

> *"Students are not greater than their teacher. But the student who is fully trained will become like the teacher."*

—Luke 6:40 (NLT)

My professional colleagues often remark about how frequently I begin a comment with, "As my grandfather used to say," or "my father told a story about…." It shows how influential their instruction was in my life. But I also recognize how often my personal preferences and behaviors mimic their lives as I observed them each day.

Making the Iron Swim

My grandfather, whom I called Papaw, was meticulous in his dress and appearance, including a carefully cultivated habit of wearing a hat. Not a baseball cap, but a real hat. My favorite picture of him was a promotional shot from his employer showing him leaning over his drafting table in the tool and die shop, metal compass in hand, looking up at a blueprint on the wall. On his head is a gorgeous gray fedora. Did he wear a hat indoors at work? I don't think so, but it made for a great picture.

Ask any friend of mine what I'm best known for in my appearance, and they will tell you about my hats. Summer, winter, casual or dressy, I'm a hat guy. Practically speaking, it fills a dual role for my bald head--warmth in the winter and shade in the summer. But for me, it's all Papaw.

I remember the morning that I realized I was shaving my father's face. Not literally, but the recognition finally dawned that while I'm a pretty good mixture of Don and Mary in my physical build, over time my face has become pure Pop. Ultimately, it's why I started growing a beard. I always admired how good one looked on his face, and felt that it was a good bet that it would work for me. For the last several years, I have sprouted some version of facial hair in the winter, and whenever I encounter folks who knew him and haven't seen me in years, I'm always pleased when they stop and exclaim, "wow, you look just like your father."

The mentoring relationship inevitably leads to some level of imitation and appropriation of word tracks, illustrations, and actions. No one expects or promotes the development of a clone, but the successful student will reflect the best parts of the mentor, such as Elisha's striking the water just as he had seen Elijah part the Jordan River.

- **Retention of unique strengths**

In light of Elisha's persistent attachment, Elijah finally asked, "what do you want from me?" (John's paraphrase), to which Elisha says, "I want to take your job and do it twice as well" (John's *really* paraphrased version). Elisha understood that an appropriation of Elijah's best traits and practices, coupled with his own strengths and abilities, would result in something even more powerful than experienced by his mentor.

I regularly comment to my friends and colleagues that I'm blessed with three incredible children, now all grown and successful, who are definite improvements on the original model. Partly because they acquired much from their mother instead of me, but also because they bring their own strengths and abilities to the table. I'm still amazed how three people born and parented in the same family can emerge as very different and unique individuals. It shows the power of mentoring and training combined with the special individual skills and traits they can cultivate as successful leaders in their respective fields.

As a *mentor*, our persistence reveals itself through:

- **Evolving roles and relationships**

Mentoring is a long-haul effort, requiring stamina to drive the relationship through a variety of competing demands on our time and complications in the process. To avoid the boredom and drudgery of mentoring as an assignment (every Tuesday for coffee, etc.), persistent mentors adjust their role with the student to reflect changing needs, as well as to recognize the multifaceted nature of leadership. Mentors may find themselves shifting from being a counselor to a guide, a tutor, or a coach as needed, which also places demands on the mentor to grow and expand their repertoire of skills. Naturally gifted talkers may need to develop more sophisticated listening skills, soft hearted counselors may need to develop a tougher coaching dimension that demands action and tangible results.

- **Thoughtful selection of students**

While I'm constantly challenging senior leaders to step up and engage in mentoring, I'm also regularly chiding some leaders to focus their mentoring time and energies more selectively. Some view group presentations, or ad hoc interactions with direct reports as mentoring, missing the intensive and transparent dimensions necessary for real leadership development. Conversely, I see some mentors who say "yes" to every request for mentoring time, spreading their energies across too many students, and leaving the mentors exhausted and the students frustrated by the thin veneer of mentoring they receive.

About ten years ago, we moved to Chicago so that I could help start a new education technology company. As with most Chicagoans, I had a 90-minute commute each way from the far western suburbs into the Loop, including an hour train ride and a

John E. Neal

six-block walk to my office. As I walked from the train station to my office, I was immediately struck by the large group of people asking for help, preferably cash. Male and female, old and young, of all varieties imaginable. But the sheer number intimidated me, while also breaking my heart.

Eventually, I consulted with a colleague about the dilemma of wanting to help, but not knowing where to start. Given her years of experience working in the Loop, she recommended that I carefully and prayerfully identify someone with whom I could make a connection, build a relationship, and hopefully find concrete ways of helping.

In the same way, we face two types of challenges as mentors: 1) we realize we can't help everyone who asks, so we help no one or, 2) we load up with as many students as possible and end up a mile wide and an inch deep in our mentoring. It's easy to discount the value of mentoring when our experiences are superficial and watered down by our lack of thoughtful selection of students.

Eventually, my daily commutes into Chicago brought me into contact with Garnett, a gentleman my age who frequented a wind-sheltered corner across from my office building. I call Garnett a gentleman, because he embodied kindness and connection in spite of his financial situation and the hustle and bustle of the commuting throng around him. Each morning and evening, you could hear Garnett's strong, deep voice carry over the roar of the street with words of welcome and encouragement to those passing by--and calling people by name once they became friends.

While I had hoped to change Garnett's life, in reality he changed mine. Homeless, jobless, often without enough money for a meal, Garnett started every conversation with questions about my life and condition.

"How's your Dad? Out of the hospital?"

"How are you handling your heavy travel schedule? Getting rest? Gwen and Caroline getting to spend time with you?"

"How long do you want to lead this company? What's your exit strategy? What's next for you?"

I'm ashamed to admit that I started my relationship with Garnett out of a sense of condescending obligation. Poor guy. I have so much and he has so little. I'll feel better if I can help him. What I quickly realized was that Garnett wasn't lazy, wasn't stupid, wasn't dirty or high or drunk. He was simply making the most of the situation in which he found himself, and wanted to be a part of something meaningful. There's no Hollywood ending to Garnett's story. Most likely, he will live his days in similar circumstances, while also continuing to connect with the people he encounters--if they are smart enough to see past his circumstances and into his heart.

- **Purposeful investment**

Anyone who's ever taken a college course from me will tell you a common "trick" I employ at the close of every class session. Regardless of the course title or class topic, I draw things to conclusion by turning to the class, spreading my hands out to my sides and raising my eyebrows. The class then says in unison, "so what?"

While it's intended to be a chuckle-inducing release from an intense time of teaching and learning, ultimately my students know that I'm asking them to draw some conclusions from the class time as they hurry on to other things. Brief moments of analysis and synthesis help us to avoid the minutiae of collecting facts and figures without an overall goal for where we're going or what we're doing with this new information or insight.

As mentors, we must remain persistent in asking ourselves and our students the "so what" question regarding our mentoring relationships. Two interrelated questions--where is this relationship going? *(desired outcomes)* and what do you want out of this mentoring time? *(benefits)*--provide the mentor with opportunities for self-assessment and student feedback to adapt, shift, or even terminate the mentoring relationship as needed. Persistent focus on the "so what" will help the mentor avoid confusing the emotion of the relationship, or the habitual repetition of the activity, with true progress in building leaders.

- **Transparent relationships**

My wife, Gwen, and I live in a condominium development in Hermitage, Tennessee, an old suburb of Nashville and home of the Andrew Jackson estate. Our condo is part of a four unit building, and we're one of the middle units, with neighbors on either side. In addition, the development features narrow streets with another building directly across, with another four units. While you might call it crowded, I believe our realtor called it intimate. I remember that descriptor, because it reminded me that we often confuse proximity with intimacy.

Just because we see one another regularly, and even share a common physical space, it doesn't mean that we know one another well, or maybe even at all. Of course, with my neighbors I fall victim to the timing issue. Once a certain period of time passes, it becomes too embarrassing to ask a neighbor their name again. So, I nod and speak and call them "neighbor" or some other substitute term.

In this passage from 2 Kings 2, Elijah and Elisha display lots of proximity--traveling together all over the region. But, Elisha's persistence ultimately leads to real transparency when Elijah finally asks, "what do you *want*?" By their very nature, mentoring relationships provide extensive opportunities for proximity. But only through persistent transparency will the mentor and student move beyond the safe emotional places and into the scary dimensions of leadership--fears, weaknesses, inadequacies, failures, and desires.

Early in my career, I volunteered for an accountability partnership with Jim at my church, which I quickly realized was a great opportunity for co-mentoring as we were both of comparable ages and career trajectories. Jim was witty, insightful, articulate, intelligent, and just plain fun to be around. Other friends would ask Jim what the color of the sky was in his world, because he lived in a completely different dimension of life--and it was infectious.

I was having a great time meeting with Jim each week, and considered myself fortunate to be his partner. But one Saturday morning at our usual coffee shop, Jim approached the table downcast and said,

"We can't be accountability partners anymore."

After the shock subsided, I asked why.

"Because I don't know who you are. You are so practiced, so expert in presenting a facade. Everything's great and you're this guy who loves God, your family, your job. Everything's perfect. I don't buy it and I can't stand it. If you can't be open and honest with me, I'm not going to waste time with you."

So, I said, "Ok, Buddy Boy, try this on for size…" and I pulled the pin on an emotional grenade I'd been carrying around. To which Jim said, "Alright then, that's a start. Let's talk." I'm not proposing that we turn the mentoring relationship into a confessional booth, but an absence of transparency leads to superficial association without the intimacy and trust built through persistent transparency.

Part Two
Building Leadership Capacity

"For unto whomsoever much is given, of him shall be much required."

—Luke 12:48 (KJV)

John E. Neal

John:

Read the preface to your book-to-be about 6:00 a.m. today. Who knew that such a short four-word statement ("make the iron swim") would make the cut after all these years, and encourage you to write a book.

You remember Wade, my old running buddy who died last May? He related this brief encounter between a preacher and an old man who was dying in an Oklahoma hospital room.

As the preacher approached the backwoodsman's bedside, the patient rumbled with a voice that seemed to come from a deep cavern. "Be ye the man of God?" The preacher said that, yes he was. The old gentleman then asked in his oh-so-bass voice, "Be ye able to make the iron swim?" Makes the hair stand up on the back of my neck just thinking about that incredible moment.

John, your preface made me weep this morning. When the time comes for you to put the book in print, if you still wish to use our special friendship and the letter about making the iron swim in the preface, I would be honored. Thank you for such a thoughtful and warm acknowledgement of the mystical connection that has been ours through the years.

An old southern cowboy, eh? Just wait till I fetch my Stetson and my squirrel rifle. Why me and old Tell Sackett might need to mosey on over to your spread and check out the brands.

All right, Pilgrim, move 'em out; you're burnin' daylight.

Jack

VI

Turning Tests into Tune Ups

"One day the widow of a member of the group of prophets came to Elisha and cried out, 'My husband who served you is dead, and you know how he feared the Lord. But now a creditor has come, threatening to take my two sons as slaves.' 'What can I do to help you?' Elisha asked, 'Tell me, what do you have in the house?' 'Nothing at all, except a flask of olive oil,' she replied.

And Elisha said, 'Borrow as many empty jars as you can from your friends and neighbors. Then go into your house with your sons and shut the door behind you. Pour olive oil from your flask into the jars, setting each one aside when it is filled.'

So she did as she was told. Her sons kept bringing jars to her, and she filled one after another.

> *Soon every container was full to the brim! 'Bring me another jar,' she said to one of her sons. 'There aren't any more!' he told her. And then the olive oil stopped flowing.*
>
> *When she told the man of God what had happened, he said to her, 'Now sell the olive oil and pay your debts, and you and your sons can live on what is left over.'"*
>
> —2 KINGS *4:1-7 (NLT)*

The fourth chapter of 2 Kings provides four different vignettes on leadership. In each story, we see Elisha expand his capacity for leadership through the circumstances encountered, while also providing his followers with glimpses of true leadership that they could then emulate and acquire for their own leadership journey.

Leading when plans fail. Media mogul Barry Diller[6] is quoted as saying, "You have an idea, and then you just put one dumb foot in front of the other and course-correct as you go." Among military leaders, the oft heard phrase is, "no battle plan survives first contact with the enemy." Plans fail. Frequently. It doesn't invalidate the value of proper planning, but an expectation that things can and will go wrong allows leaders to anticipate and cultivate the capacity to lead teams through the uncertainty of change.

---

6 Timothy Ferriss (2017) *Tribe of Mentors: Short Life Advice from the Best in the World.* New York: Houghton Mifflin Harcourt.

Making the Iron Swim

"One day Elisha went to the town of Shunem. A wealthy woman lived there, and she urged him to come to her home for a meal. After that, whenever he passed that way, he would stop there for something to eat.

Later Elisha asked Gehazi, 'What can we do for her?' Gehazi replied. 'She doesn't have a son, and her husband is an old man.' 'Call her back again,' Elisha told him. When the woman returned, Elisha said to her as she stood in the doorway, 'Next year at this time you will be holding a son in your arms!' 'No, my lord!' she cried. 'O man of God, don't deceive me and get my hopes up like that.' But sure enough, the woman soon become pregnant. And at that time the following year she had a son, just as Elisha had said.

One day when her child was older, he went out to help his father, who was working with the harvesters. Suddenly he cried out, 'My head hurts! My head hurts!' His father said to one of the servants, 'Carry him home to his mother.' So the servant took him home, and his mother held him on her lap. But around noontime he died. She carried him up and laid him on the bed of the man of God, then shut the door and left him there.

But when she came to the man of God at the mountain, she fell to the ground before him and caught hold of his feet. Gehazi began to push her away, but the man of God said, 'Leave her alone. She is deeply troubled, but the Lord has not told me what it is.' Then she said, 'Did I ask you for a son, my lord? And didn't I say, Don't deceive me and get my hopes up?'

When Elisha arrived, the child was indeed dead, lying there on the prophet's bed. He went in alone and shut the door behind him and prayed to the Lord. Then he lay down on the child's body, placing his mouth on the child's mouth, his eyes on the child's eyes, and his hands on the child's hands. And as he stretched out on him, the child's body began to grow warm again!

Then Elisha summoned Gehazi. 'Call the child's mother!' he said. And when she came in, Elisha said, 'Here, take your son!' She fell at his feet and bowed before him, overwhelmed with gratitude. Then she took her son in her arms and carried him downstairs."

—2 KINGS *4: 8, 14-23, 27-28, 32-34, 36-37*
(NLT)

Leading when hopes are crushed. The longer the wait, the bigger the hope, the greater the opportunity for deep despair and heartache. While not on the same emotional level as a lifelong hope for a child, many leaders carry an aspiration for leadership, or for the development of an organization for decades before seeing it come to fruition. Which brings the potential for catastrophic emotional damage when plans go awry, or when our laser-like drive for success in that long-awaited venture leads to unhealthy or destructive decisions. Great leaders develop leaders within their organizations, including the opportunity to dream their own dreams and pursue ambitious opportunities. Sometimes those hopes are crushed and mentors must help resurrect life from the dying corpse of a dream.

> *"Elisha now returned to Gilgal, and there was a famine in the land. One day as the group of prophets was seated before him, he said to his servant, 'Put a large pot on the fire, and make some stew for the rest of the group.'*
>
> *One of the young men went out into the field to gather herbs and came back with a pocketful of wild gourds. He shredded them and put them into the pot without realizing they were poisonous. Some of the stew was served to the men. But after they had eaten a bite or two they cried out, 'Man of God, there's poison in this stew!' So they would not eat it.*

John E. Neal

> *Elisha said, 'Bring me some flour.' Then he threw it into the pot and said, 'Now it's all right; go ahead and eat.' And then it did not harm them.*
>
> —*2 Kings 4:38-41 (NLT)*

Leading when people make poor choices. Effective leadership runs counter to the human bias that "if you want something done right, do it yourself." Great leaders empower people to take initiative, often with the hope of finding better ways of getting things done. The practice of delegation, however, is doubly difficult (a) because we have a tough time allowing people to do the "highly important" tasks that we reserve for ourselves and (b) because they mess them up regularly. If you don't want to clean up messes, don't be a leader.

My friend John founded a church in a medium-sized metropolitan area and helped lead it to significant growth. Early in the church planting stage, John's church hosted a day care center in the educational wing of their recently leased building. Prior to the leasing of the building, no one told John that a combination of environmental factors made the classroom wing a perfect breeding ground for black flies. Not an ideal location for children.

So, every morning prior to the arrival of teachers and students, John would roll up a magazine and stroll the hall swatting flies and sweeping up the results. In seminary, no one told John that founding pastors would have to be the exterminators du jour. But, great leaders roll up their sleeves and clean up the messes.

Making the Iron Swim

"One day a man from Baal-shalishah brought the man of God a sack of fresh grain and twenty loaves of barley bread made from the first grain of the harvest. Elisha said, 'Give it to the people so they can eat.' 'What?' his servant exclaimed. 'Feed a hundred people with only this?'

But Elisha repeated, 'Give it to the people so that they can eat, for this is what the Lord says: Everyone will eat, and there will even be some left over!' And when they gave it to the people, there was plenty for all and some left over, just as the Lord had promised.'

—2 Kings 4: 42-44 (NLT)

Leading when needs outstrip resources. I have yet to meet a manager or leader who said that they had ample resources to accomplish their goals, thank you very much. While planning sets a direction, prioritization defines a process for implementing the direction and exposes our values as leaders in terms of fairness and equity. This is an age of the "self made" person, justifying the self-serving business plan of start it, sell it, and retire comfortably.

Great leaders place people before personal advancement, and understand that employees come before customers. If leaders don't treat their own people well, how can they build a business that serves strangers effectively? Steven Sample, the former president of the University of Southern California, observed that many people want to *be* a college president, but very few of them want to *do* president:

> *"Some of the unhappiest people I know are those whose aspirations for a high-level leadership position were finally satisfied, and who only then found out that they didn't really want to do what it is that the position required. They had spent years clawing and scraping their way up the mountain, and upon reaching their goal discovered that the realities of life at the top were a far cry from what they had imagined them to be."*[7]

Leading is a messy, emotionally taxing journey, requiring the development of skills and behaviors that reassure the team and enable thoughtful responses to crises.

Be the leader your team needs in a crisis. When the crisis appears--and it will appear at the most perfectly inopportune moment--the leader's initial actions and reactions will set the tone for the rest of the team and either build trust and security for the organization or pour gasoline on the smoldering embers of the crisis--allowing it to erupt into a full-scale disaster.

- **Hit the pause button.** Fight the temptation to do something immediately--what some call the "ready, fire, aim approach"--which includes emails, phone calls, or public pronouncements. During this initial period, a minute

---

[7] Steven B. Sample (2002) *The Contrarian's Guide to Leadership.* San Francisco: Jossey-Bass.

will feel like an hour and an hour like a day, but speed to action is not your friend. Remember Solomon's wisdom: *"Even fools are thought wise when they keep silent; with their mouths shut, they seem intelligent."* (Proverbs 17:28 NLT)

- **Ask for help.** I used to think that only newer or younger leaders struggled with the fear of being seen as inexperienced, uncertain, or unseasoned. But we all dislike being seen as needy or unprepared or uninformed. Experienced leaders display their quiet assurance best when they ask for contributions from others. And team members who have been consulted for ideas buy into final plans more fully and enthusiastically.
- **Suspend final judgment.** Avoid listening only to your trusted advisors (or only to yourself) which merely reinforces your existing perceptions and biases. Seek out fresh perspectives and approaches. My grandfather regularly warned me against what he called "the deadliest combination" of arrogance and ignorance. Either characteristic--not knowing or not caring about other ideas--damages our ability to lead during crises, and the combination provides a toxic brew that will scuttle organizations.
- **Follow the plan.** Once a proposed solution is finalized and executed, don't grow faint at the first sign of complaint or opposition. Properly vetted strategies often take time to find traction in addressing the problem. Give it time, and reassure your colleagues. Bouncing from one solution to another will dismay your staff and empower your opponents.

- **Aspire to be seen as a "sufficient" leader, not a Superhero.** In an era of superlatives (great, premier, top tier), leaders often aim for unrealistic legacies that result in demoralizing cultures, especially during difficult times. Of course, our organizations preface this preoccupation with extraordinariness by writing job descriptions for leadership positions that appear to have been written by Stan Lee (creator of Marvel comics): able to leap tall buildings, faster than a speeding bullet, more powerful than a locomotive. And, yes, I know those describe Superman, which is a DC comic. I'm a nerd, too. However, for our employees and colleagues, "sufficient" leadership displays a different set of characteristics each day:
  - **Be there.** Don't disappear during a crisis. Stay engaged.
  - **Be dependable.** Remember the old saying, "Say what you mean and mean what you say?" Not everyone in an organization will know everything that's going on, but what they know should be the truth. And if the information or outcome changes, they will know in a timely way and with an explanation of why things changed.
  - **Be calm in a crisis.** The last person in the world we want to see with their hair on fire or out of control is the leader. Get a grip and encourage it in others.
  - **Banish the 110% myth.** There are only so many hours in a day, days in a week, etc. Nothing demoralizes staff more than the notion that this plan or project or company will only succeed if I give an unrealistic sustained effort to the task. Cultivate the

concepts of "achievable," "sustainable," and "balanced" in your organizational rhetoric and planning.

Become the seasoned leader your team emulates. During a restructuring of a company in which I served in a leadership role, we moved to new offices a few blocks away. The senior team gathered in my old office with the floor plan of the new building, revealing an "L" shaped working space, and my office in the corner with floor to ceiling glass walls. I remarked that the layout would facilitate my ability to keep an eye on things. But one of the senior members of the team countered with, "Oh, no. We're putting you in the middle so that everyone can keep an eye on you. We'll be watching every move you make. When you arrive and leave. How you dress. How you interact with people. Will the door remain closed or will your office be a meeting space? You'll be setting the tone for the entire company." Gulp.

- **Identify the familiar road signs.** For seasoned leaders, the current crisis is not your first rodeo, first space shot, first lap around the race track (pick your favorite). I love the movie scene in *Apollo 13* during take-off when Commander James Lovell (played by Tom Hanks) quietly and calmly talks the crew through the various stages of ascent. During stressful moments, don't merely recognize the familiar warning signs and issue orders. Help your less experienced colleagues recognize the issues at hand, both to help them develop their own repertoire of reactive skills, and to build trust in your perspective and calm action under pressure.

- **Avoid bitterness and cynicism.** Familiarity with the stressful parts of a position can also breed contempt within a leader. "Been there, done that" often leads to boredom and disdain, magnifying the minor irritations of the position into a toxic mindset that will infect your colleagues and contaminate the organization's culture.
- **Keep an open mind.** I regularly espouse the 80-20 rule of leadership. Most of what seasoned leaders encounter (about 80%) is familiar from prior work experience, while some smaller percentage (around 20%) represents undiscovered territory that will either bring breakthrough opportunities or provide interesting ways to derail or destroy momentum and credibility. The key challenge? Recognize and differentiate between the 80 and the 20 and perform appropriately by knowing when to hold fast and when to adapt and adjust. An executive colleague once remarked that the danger of hiring seasoned leaders in new organizations or new roles resides in finding the correct balance between these two categories. Enter the company or position with a "been there, done that, got a t-shirt" smirk, and you'll alienate people who may have discovered a better approach. Conversely, tip-toe into the new team with a blank stare and a "I'm just here to learn" mantra, and your colleagues will wonder why the organization hired a supposed leader. We all develop a leadership bag of tricks along the way. One that fits our style, approach and context. It's one of the reasons we've enjoyed a level of success up to this point. But,

realizing that the bag of tricks is not finite, fixed, or sufficient gives us continued opportunities to lead and grow simultaneously.

- **Recognize successes and celebrate blessings.** On a number of personality profiles, I regularly land on the dividing line between two categories, the introvert-extrovert dimension. I don't know if that makes me an introverted extrovert or an extroverted introvert, but the absence of a clear result allows me to empathize with colleagues who fit cleanly in each category and who respond differently to various approaches to recognition and motivation. Attend any big company meeting and observe the division of the universe at work. Extroverts close to the stage whooping with delight at high energy events, while introverts line the back wall looking for an exit. Some employees need and want the awards hanging in their cubicle. Others want a quiet word of thanks and a brief note of appreciation in the company newsletter. Regardless of the approach, it's vital that we take time to recognize our successes (achieving things we had hoped and planned to achieve) and celebrate our blessings (receiving happy surprises along the way). Sometimes our careful planning and hard work pay off as hoped. Other times, we are the recipients of just dumb luck—or divine grace. Lead your colleagues in recognizing and celebrating both.

John E. Neal

John,

You're Alive!

So good to hear from you. I've been praying for you, and I think of you as I move through the day dodging deadlines. You'll always be loved, always be appreciated, always mentioned with respect at my house.

Six months of unemployment...and a door opens. Thank the Lord for this new opportunity. Just eighteen short months ago, I experienced three months of disorienting unemployment and two more months of half-time employment. So I understand some of what you've been experiencing. We're still digging out from that financial disaster. You know this road.

And I'm not surprised to hear that God is working in and through you as you step away from the hurt and despair. What a dark night you've traveled, my friend. I cried out for you many days in the wee hours alone in my living room, believing that God would stand by you in the heartache and disappointment.

Gotta shut down and go to yet another meeting tonight. But before I do, I wanted you to know that your email is an answer to my prayers. Remember that you're loved.

Jack

VII
Facing Challenges

As a child of the 60s, I remember each Christmas season hearing and singing the classic song, "Let There Be Peace On Earth"[8]:

> *"Let there be peace on Earth,*
> *And let it begin with me..."*

Even though it wasn't originally conceived as a Christmas song, it became a staple of the season, as thoughts centered on peace as represented by the Prince of Peace. In the maelstrom of leadership, those words have inspired me during difficult, contentious and confrontational moments. If I'm to find a way of de-escalating the moment, it must start with me.

---

8 Jill Jackson-Miller & Sy Miller (1983) *Let There Be Peace On Earth.* Jan-Lee Music.

Similarly, the leadership classic, *Leadership and Self-Deception*[9], reminds us that self-deception leads us to destructive decisions, because we can't see how we're the problem. My favorite passage occurs within the preface of the book:

> *"Self-deception is like this. It blinds us to the true causes of problems, and once we're blind, all the 'solutions' we can think of will actually make matters worse. Whether at work or at home, self-deception obscures the truth about ourselves, corrupts our view of others and our circumstances, and inhibits our ability to make wise and helpful decisions."*

So, take a fresh glimpse of your organizational value statements, the ones that grace the walls of your office, website, and employee orientation materials. And let it begin with you…

But, there are other people involved in the difficult issue at hand, with three common challenges as illustrated by Elisha:

1. Dealing with Resistance to Change

> *"The king of Aram had great admiration for Naaman, the commander of his army, because through him the Lord had given Aram great victories. But though Naaman was a mighty warrior, he suffered from leprosy. At this time Aramean raiders had invaded the land of Israel, and among*

---

[9] The Arbinger Institute (2010) *Leadership and Self-Deception: Getting Out of the Box*. Oakland: Berrett-Koehler Publishers.

Making the Iron Swim

their captives was a young girl who had been given to Naaman's wife as a maid. One day the girl said to her mistress, 'I wish my master would go see the prophet in Samaria. He would heal him of his leprosy.'

So Naaman went with his horses and chariots and waited at the door of Elisha's house. But Elisha sent a messenger out to him with this message: 'Go and wash yourself seven times in the Jordan River. Then your skin will be restored and you will be healed of your leprosy.' But Naaman became angry and stalked away. 'I thought he would certainly come out to meet me!' he said. 'I expected him to wave his hand over the leprosy and call on the name of the Lord his God and heal me! Aren't the rivers of Damascus, the Albana and the Pharpar, better than any of the rivers of Israel? Why shouldn't I wash in them and be healed?' So Naaman turned and went away in a rage.

But his officers tried to reason with him and said, 'Sir, if the prophet had told you to do something very difficult, wouldn't you have done it? So you should certainly obey him when he says simply, Go and wash and be cured!' So Naaman went down to the Jordan River and dipped himself seven times, as the man of God had instructed him. And

> *his skin became as healthy as the skin of a young child, and he was healed!"*
>
> —2 KINGS 5: 1-3; 9-14 (NLT)

If we're honest with ourselves, we know deep inside that we hate change. Yup, I said hate. I know it's not fashionable or career-enhancing to say it. We're supposed to embrace it, drive it, celebrate it. But, often, we hate it. Your coffee shop stops carrying your favorite blend, your new cell phone requires a swipe up instead of a swipe down, your kids don't want you to kiss them good-night anymore because they're too old and sophisticated. Your boss shows up with the newest strategic plan and the performance standards that equate to keeping your job or maintaining your expected level of income.

As someone who has worked in the online learning/education technology sphere for many years, I see first-hand the challenges of leading change at colleges and universities. And, because it happens to be change that I embrace, drive, and celebrate, I just can't understand why some people can't go with the flow. Why do they hate change so much? John Kotter's foundational work, *Leading Change*[10], provides thoughtful context for this resistance:

> *"People who have been through difficult, painful, and not very successful change efforts often end up drawing both pessimistic and angry conclusions. They become suspicious of*

---

10 John P. Kotter (1996) *Leading Change.* Boston: Harvard Business School Press.

the motives of those pushing for transformation; they worry that major change is not possible without carnage; they fear that the boss is a monster or that much of the management is incompetent."

The story of Elisha and Naaman helps illustrate key dimensions leaders must address to overcome resistance to change.

- **Broken Dreams**--By all accounts, Naaman was a successful military leader. But our perception of his success may not align with his prior dreams and aspirations. Often the people in our organizations that fight change the hardest are "successful" in our eyes, but harbor very different expectations of where they wanted to be at this stage in their lives. They want to say to us, "you're not happy with where we are? Well, I'm not happy either!"
- **Unfulfilled Promises**--I'm sure that Naaman received lots of suggestions over the years to address his physical ailment. Failure after failure led him to be cynical about new ideas. Our employees have been burned by past leaders and previous plans for innovation and change. "Been there, done that" could be emblazoned on every shirt worn at your place of work. Most of it cost people time, effort, sweat and tears. And changed little over the long haul. They may not see themselves as pessimistic about change (Kotter's term), but they are definitely cautious. My grandmother attended the same little country church for 70 years. She sat in the same seat in the same pew and watched ministers come and go, while attendance

fluctuated between 75-150 people. Her attitude, while not resistant to change, sums up the unspoken position of your colleagues--"I was here long before the new leader arrived, and I'll be here long after he/she leaves."

- **Lack of Urgency**--Was Naaman content to have leprosy? Of course not. Even though the Arameans followed a different societal code for those who suffered from the debilitating skin disease (the Israelites banished those with the malady), Naaman's chronic condition affected his life and future in significant ways. And yet, as time passes Naaman becomes accustomed to the situation, resulting in a lack of urgency to address the issue. In our organizations, we readily see the obvious issues needing to be addressed and changed. But our colleagues have seen it for so long, they have grown accustomed to them and no longer notice. As a college president, I would invite presidential colleagues to visit me on campus for lunch and a walk of the facilities and grounds. My simple request was for them to point out the obvious issues requiring my time and action. Frequently, the items highlighted by my colleagues were things I had noticed early in my tenure, but had grown weary in addressing, and eventually became numb to their presence. Change requires a renewed sense of urgency.

- **Arrogance**--A variation of the "I'm not the problem" self-deception, where we only listen to our inner voices and those of our closest confidants. If I didn't think of the solution, it's suspect. Notice the personal pronouns in Naaman's angry outbursts. "This isn't the way I would do

it," "why are we listening to you and not to me?" Change forces us to listen to new (and challenging) views.
- **Powerlessness**--The ultimate destination for our employees and colleagues when circumstances require drastic change. "I've tried in the past and it didn't work, and no matter what I do, nothing changes." Naaman's anger emerges from that dark place. Trying something new and then failing only deepens the despair. So better to complain, critique, and resist than to try and fail and feel hopeless and helpless.

2. Dealing with Disobedience/Dishonesty

> *"Then Naaman and his entire party went back to find the man of God. They stood before him, and Naaman said, 'Now I know that there is no God in all the world except in Israel. So please accept a gift from your servant.' But Elisha replied, 'As surely as the Lord lives, whom I serve, I will not accept any gifts.'*
>
> *But Gehazi, the servant of Elisha, the man of God, said to himself, 'My master should not have let this Aramean get away without accepting any of his gifts. As surely as the Lord lives, I will chase after him and get something from him.' So Gehazi set off after Naaman.*
>
> *When Naaman saw Gehazi running after him, he climbed down from his chariot and went to meet*

> *him. 'Is everything all right?' Naaman asked. 'Yes,' Gehazi said, 'but my master has sent me to tell you that two young prophets from the hill country of Ephraim have just arrived. He would like 75 pounds of silver and two sets of clothing to give to them.'*
>
> *'By all means, take twice as much silver,' Naaman insisted. He gave him two sets of clothing, tied up the money in two bags, and sent two of his servants to carry the gifts for Gehazi. But when they arrived at the Citadel, Gehazi took the gifts from the servants and sent the men back. Then he went and hid the gifts inside the house.*
>
> *When he went in to his master, Elisha asked him, 'Where have you been, Gehazi?' 'I haven't been anywhere,' he replied."*
>
> —2 KINGS 5: 15-16A; 20-25 (NLT)

Hire well. The first piece of advice I was given as a brand-new supervisor. First the good news--we have an open position to fill. Then comes the agonizing process of finding the best candidate. We hire search firms to compile vetted groups of highly-gifted candidates, we interview and interview *ad nauseum* to avoid a hasty decision, and we check multiple references for background and accuracy in the candidate's resume and experiences. Then something catastrophic happens.

Evidently, Gehazi had served Elisha for a while. He knew his master's wishes and preferences. His identity was tied up with that of his employer, "the servant of Elisha, the man of God." And yet, in the heat of the moment, he made a catastrophic choice--and lied about it. While we and our colleagues avoid the severe consequences suffered by Gehazi (he was cursed with the leprosy from which Naaman had been cured), our moral lapses and the dishonesty that usually accompanies them creates embarrassment and damage for our lives, our loved ones, our colleagues, and our organizations.

Gehazi illustrates three characteristics that remain all too common for us and even our best employees:

- **Deception**--In this continuing theme of self-deception, Gehazi was so convinced of Elisha's short-sightedness in refusing financial reward, he blinded himself to the larger moral issue. I work hard, I deserve it. Everyone else does something worse, this is a small thing. No one will know. I've got this under control.
- **Impersonation**--As a young professional working for a university president, I needed to be reminded regularly that I represented the president at meetings, but that I didn't speak for him, nor was I a quasi-president in my own right. Sometimes I was a messenger, taking a verbatim answer from my boss. Other times, I would sit in on a meeting and give an opinion of how the president might respond to a situation. But, I entered dangerous territory whenever my ego led me to think, "I'm so close to the president, I can speak for him, because I know

what he would want, or should decide about an issue." Gehazi assumed the mantle of Elisha in his representations. Disaster resulted.
- **Foolishness**--In the Bible, the term "fool" is a moral designation. It's not the same thing as dumb or stupid or uneducated. If a wise person applies learning at the right time, a fool applies his well practiced bad behavior at the worst possible moment. I'm taking liberties with the Biblical story, but Gehazi didn't think this scenario up all at once. His disobedience and deception were the product of practiced thoughts and actions.

3. Picking Up the Pieces

"One day the group of prophets came to Elisha and told him, 'As you can see, this place where we meet with you is too small. Let's go down to the Jordan River, where there are plenty of logs. There we can build a new place for us to meet.'

'All right,' he told them, 'go ahead.'

'Please come with us,' someone suggested.

'I will,' he said. So he went with them. When they arrived at the Jordan, they began cutting down trees. But as one of them was cutting a tree, his ax head fell into the river. 'Oh, sir!' he cried. 'It was a borrowed ax!'

Making the Iron Swim

> *'Where did it fall?' the man of God asked. When he showed him the place, Elisha cut a stick and threw it into the water at that spot. Then the ax head floated to the surface. 'Grab it,' Elisha said. And the man reached out and grabbed it."*
>
> —2 KINGS 6:1-7 (NLT)

Initiative. We encourage it, we hire for it, we reward it. But, it comes with a price. Bumps in the road. Imperfect outcomes. Embarrassing blunders. Sometimes the problems are minor and easily fixed. Sometimes they are career threatening for your team member and for you as their leader. In this title story, we easily discount the scope of the drama. An ax head was someone's career, their way of making a living. Loaned in good faith and now sitting at the bottom of the Jordan River. While I've never been able to perform a feat of supernatural proportions, Elisha's example provides context for our leadership responsibility to clean up after our folks when things go wrong:

- **Encourage Initiative**--Our colleagues will see things that need addressing long before we do, and they will bring us ideas and solutions before they become items on our "to-do" list. We don't have to say yes to every idea or suggestion that appears, but the best way to kill initiative is to say no frequently and condescendingly.
- **Don't Micromanage**--It's their idea, their proposed solution to a problem. Let them sit and soak with it. Let them draft and refine and debate. The group of prophets

mentioned in this story were actually students in a school training to be the next generation of spiritual leaders for Israel. A favorite parlor game of college presidents is to share the wacky ideas that emanate from the student government association. Of course, some of the best ideas for campus improvements also come from this group. Give people a chance to learn to discern the difference.

- **Stick Around**--Just because it isn't your idea and you don't want to micromanage, don't disappear and bail on the initiative. My favorite phrase in this passage is "please come with us." Those should be sweet words in the ears of any leader. They want you around when they are attempting something new and intimidating. And avoid the verbal and non-verbal cues that would turn this into how you would do it. Presence is not supervision.
- **Work a "Miracle" When Needed**--As a consultant, my phone most often rings when something has gone wrong. In my personal lexicon, I differentiate between an "oops" and a "hairball." An "oops" usually requires a suggestion or two, while a "hairball" necessitates an intervention--and sometimes prayer and fasting to address! Focus on Elisha in this story. No emotional outburst, no tongue lashing of the student, no disappearing at the critical moment. This wasn't Elisha's first time to solve a big problem. As seasoned leaders, we need to bring that same portfolio of skills to our sudden hairballs. Suck out the emotion from the room, refrain from placing blame, and solve the problem the best way you know from experience. Trust me, your people will view it as miraculous.

Making the Iron Swim

I was fortunate to grow up around the corner from Kent, who went from high school basketball star to college star to a career in the NBA. Having a basketball goal on our garage enabled me to watch Kent shoot hook shots for hours and hours. Years later, Gwen and I were living in the Detroit area and were able to watch Kent play for the Pistons. In the middle of the game, Kent crossed the key, took the pass, turned slightly and let the ball arc off of his fingers, high above the outstretched hands trying to block his shot. As the ball swished through the net, I heard someone in our section remark, "how does he do that?" My first thought was of that garage goal and the hours of practice. It wasn't his first time to let the shot fly in a pressure-filled situation. As leaders, we should practice picking up the pieces and supporting our people so that when the hairballs appear, we won't be taking the pressure shot for the first time. Your miracle making will encourage the kind of initiative that will also appear miraculous.

John E. Neal

John,

Thanks a million for the warm and thoughtful letter. You're covered up with relocation details, learning a new role and finding balance in a whirling educational stew. And still you made time to write.

Thanks, John, you're a special man. I'm so glad our lives intersect from time to time along the way.

If you're like the prophet Elisha, you're only required to make the iron swim once in order for the work to proceed. Now that you know you can trust God in doing that impossible task, you'll know what to expect when the next impossible assignment lands on your plate and you're asked to walk on water. Jesus did it because it needed to be done, apparently thought there was nothing unusual about the tactic, and taught Peter how to do it in a storm without any previous practice.

Umm, for what it's worth, walking on water is only necessary in a life-or-death crisis with the winds high and the waves rough. Most of the time, God permits His servants to use oars, small boats with sails or pieces of wrecked vessels (in the case of the Apostle Paul) to get where they need to go.

You will recall that the prophet didn't seem surprised that the iron swam, nor was Jesus surprised when Peter stepped out of the boat and did not sink. I wonder why it is that God always uses our storms to teach us new truths…

Jack

Part III
Leaving a Legacy

"Remember your leaders who taught you the Word of God. Think of all the good that has come from their lives, and follow the example of their faith."

—Hebrews 13:7 (NLT)

VIII

The Vision Thing

It's tough to be the heir apparent, especially when you're following a strong and dynamic leader, or working in close proximity to one when comparisons are inevitable. Some leaders naturally evoke such a strong sense of personal presence and institutional direction that those following in the role can be swamped in the wake of their charisma. President Reagan left such a void for his Vice President and successor.

During the 1988 presidential campaign of George H. W. Bush, *Time* magazine ran an article by Robert Ajemian entitled, "Where is the Real George Bush?[11]" Ajemian wrote:

"Colleagues say that while Bush understands thoroughly the complexities of issues, he does not easily fit them into larger themes. This has led to the charge that he lacks vision. It rankles him. Recently he asked a friend to help him identify some cutting issues for next year's campaign. Instead, the

---

11 Robert Ajemian (January 26, 1987) "Where Is The Real George Bush?" *Time*.

> *friend suggested that Bush go alone to Camp David for a few days to figure out where he wanted to take the country. 'Oh,' said Bush in clear exasperation, 'the vision thing.' The friend's advice did not impress him."*

Elisha's leadership displays extraordinary vision in marked contrast to the visionless commands of the king of Aram.

> *"When the king of Aram was at war with Israel, he would confer with his officers and say, 'We will mobilize our forces at such and such a place.'*
>
> *But immediately, Elisha, the man of God, would warn the king of Israel, 'Do not go near that place, for the Arameans are planning to mobilize their troops there.' So the king of Israel would send word to the place indicated by the man of God. Time and again Elisha warned the king, so that he would be on the alert there.*
>
> *The king of Aram became very upset over this. He called his officers together and demanded, 'Which of you is the traitor? Who has been informing the king of Israel of my plans?'*
>
> *'It's not us, my lord the king,' one of the officers replied. 'Elisha, the prophet of Israel, tells the king of Israel even the words you speak in the privacy of your bedroom!'*

Making the Iron Swim

> *'Go and find out where he is,' the king commanded, 'so I can send troops to seize him.' And the report came back: 'Elisha is at Dothan.' So one night the king of Aram sent a great army with many chariots and horses to surround the city.*
>
> *When the servant of the man of God got up early the next morning and went outside, there were troops, horses, and chariots everywhere. 'Oh sir, what will we do now?' the young man cried to Elisha.*
>
> *'Don't be afraid!' Elisha told him. 'For there are more on our side than on theirs!' Then Elisha prayed, 'O LORD, open his eyes and let him see!' The LORD opened the young man's eyes, and when he looked up, he saw the hillside around Elisha was filled with horses and chariots of fire."*
>
> —2 KINGS 6:8-17 (NLT)

The Visionless Leader

- **Predictable**--Not "predictable" in the stable, consistent sense of the word, but "predictable" in the boring, habitual sense that returns to the same well-worn paths over and over, so that colleagues and employees can predict your response and direction. For emotionally-driven leaders, there's an additional layer of "predictable unpredictability". When the leader is in a good mood, certain things happen (or don't happen) and vice versa. So team members learn to stockpile difficult pieces of information or requests waiting for the leader's change in mood. I'm not advocating wildly swinging styles in leadership, but once your people can accurately anticipate your reactions, requests, and directions, you become a useless step in the organization's operation.

- **Reactionary**--Once Elisha began to successfully anticipate and counteract the King's military advantage, the King started looking for a scapegoat. Clearly, the only rational explanation for these repeated failures was some traitorous, backbiting, ungrateful insider. Or so thought the King. I find the one constant and repeating leadership theme of Elisha's life to be the reality of failure. And yet, even seasoned executives often seem surprised by failure, and react in childish or thoughtless ways when failure inevitably occurs. Our employees pay careful attention to our actions, but they acquire laser-like focus on our reactions to failure, seeing if or when we contradict our public narrative of team with our private reactions that point blame and seek vengeance.
- **Clueless**--I can't help but chuckle each time I read this story about Elisha and the King. The King finds himself outwitted by Elisha repeatedly, but once his officers convince him of Elisha's espionage, he orders his troops to ascertain Elisha's location so that they can go capture him. As if this time Elisha will be apprehended.

It reminds me of visionless leaders who latch onto an idea and keep forcing the organization through another attempt to execute the plan, believing this time they will succeed. You've seen teams sitting around a table as the leader pushes a pet project over and over. And harder and harder. The non-verbal communication in the room--heads bowed, eyes rolling, arms crossed--screams silently "not again, have you lost your mind?" And yet, we are all clueless at some point about that "brilliant" idea that was merely poorly funded or not executed well. If we would just try harder this time, we would have a better outcome. And so the eyes start rolling...

The Visionary Leader

- **Anticipates**--Apparently, one of my favorite leadership quotes from the sports world is overused. My Canadian friends are tired of consultants and companies quoting Wayne Gretzky[12]: "A good hockey player plays where the puck is. A great hockey player plays where the puck is going to be." But, it's my book, and I like it. Visionary leaders don't consult a crystal ball or have a sixth sense. They learn to pay attention to the field of play, using their personal portfolio of experiences--both good and bad--that allow them to see important developments ahead,

---

[12] Jason Kirby (October 3, 2014) "CEOs: Stop Debasing Wayne Gretzky's Quote" *Canadian Business*.

whether they are opportunities to pursue or threats to avoid. While it's easy to associate vision exclusively with forward movement and action, anticipation also includes the critical concept of patience, of observant expectation, that values timing as much as direction. Elisha knew where to go (or where to avoid), but the timing of those movements was the critical factor in his success.

- **Identifies Hidden Resources**--I particularly enjoy the moment in this Bible passage when Elisha prays that God would open his servant's eyes. It makes me wonder how many times my bosses or colleagues over the years have prayed that I would wake up or pay closer attention to events going on around me. My ninth-grade basketball coach especially enjoyed screaming "wake up, Neal!" On a regular basis. But, beyond his divinely enabled observational skills (which would be incredibly helpful for any leader), Elisha's story illustrates the necessary ability of visionary leaders to find and deploy resources unnoticed by others. Major corporations today spend unprecedented levels on human resources management, while simultaneously, people often feel invisible within their own organizations. Obviously, mid- to lower-level staff members within a large organization wouldn't expect the CEO to call them by name, unless their paths crossed regularly. But, they would expect their immediate supervisor and their supervisor's supervisor to have a clear sense of their role, their abilities, and their contributions to the success and future growth of the company. And they have every right to expect it. A colleague once related to me his three separate "first-time" introductions to the CEO. Painful and awkward, but not fatal. More troubling is our tendency as leaders to become oblivious to our most important resource--our people--which feeds employee dissatisfaction and turnover. Human resource management is so much more than hiring, firing, and benefits. Building a team with the future in mind and then building our people to succeed in those roles will generate the kind of employee loyalty and longevity that sets our organization apart and creates positive buzz in our competitive sphere. And in the pressure-filled moments, when the future of our organization may hang in the balance, our ability to survey the horizon and see the wonderful people we've placed on our team will be the critical difference between terror and confidence.

- **Unpredictable**--In stark contrast to the Visionless Leader's annoying predictability, the Visionary Leader brings a fresh perspective to the issues and challenges at hand by recharging and retooling on an ongoing basis. Whether you like to read, listen to audiobooks, watch Ted lectures online, or attend professional conferences, the investment of new information--coupled with an open mind to differing perspectives--will enable the Visionary Leader to reexamine long-held beliefs and biases about strategic direction and chronic challenges. Rather than being seen as wishy-washy or uncertain, a leader's ability to revise positions and recalibrate policies, procedures and products will embolden teammates and employees to reassess their own activities and decisions. When we only listen to advice from "trusted" sources that reinforce our current position (as with the king in this story), we blind ourselves to the broader range of options that may include our best solution to our current dilemma.

IX
Ending Well

A friend of mine attended a track and field event at the local middle school. A young man who lived in his neighborhood was competing in the mile run, and was easily leading the pack for the first three laps. Then, halfway through lap four, the boy suddenly turned left and cut directly through the football field to the finish line. While the young man technically finished first, he actually finished last after his disqualification. My colleague rushed to the youngster and asked what in the world caused him to do such a thing. The boy simply replied, "I got tired."

Leadership over a lifetime requires the stamina of a marathoner, rather than a sprinter. Most of a leader's goals are long-term, and the leadership lexicon is more strategic than immediate. A colleague who enjoyed an unusually long tenure as a college president once remarked that he didn't feel any significant traction and movement in his job until after ten years. Unfortunately, that's an experience most university presidents will never know, since the average tenure is less than five years.

My favorite music teacher shared his secret to a successful performance, especially a long composition played by struggling beginners. "Start well and end well, and the audience will forget everything in the middle." That's sage advice for any leader facing another lap on the track. How we finish is as important as how we start. I'm intentionally using the same Elisha passage here at the end as I used at the beginning, only starting earlier in the narrative to give broader context.

> *"When Elisha was in his last illness, King Jehoash of Israel visited him and wept over him. 'My father! My father! I see the chariots and charioteers of Israel!' He cried. Elisha told him, 'Get a bow and some arrows.' And the king did as he was told. Elisha told him, 'Put your hand on the bow,' and Elisha laid his own hands on the King's hands.*
>
> *The he commanded, 'Open that eastern window,' and he opened it. Then he said, 'Shoot!" So he shot an arrow. Elisha proclaimed, 'This is the Lord's arrow, an arrow of victory over Aram, for you will completely conquer the Arameans at Aphek.'*
>
> *Then Elisha died and was buried.*
>
> *Groups of Moabite raiders used to invade the land each spring. Once when some Israelites were burying a man, they spied a band of these raiders.*

Making the Iron Swim

> *So they hastily threw the corpse into the tomb of Elisha and fled. But as soon as the body touched Elisha's bones, the dead man revived and jumped to his feet!"*

—2 KINGS 13:14-17; 20-21 (NLT)

In this, the final story of Elisha's life, we see in dramatic fashion the common challenges facing all leaders, but especially those who erroneously believed that merely achieving a specific role or title would make them a leader, and so they cut the corner to the finish:

- **Feeling powerless within the constraints of the position**

    When I was a very young president of a small college in a rural community, I was invited to serve on a conference panel with the chancellor of the flagship state university just up the road. We were both invited by a major foundation to answer questions on higher education leadership from differing perspectives (large vs. small university, older vs. younger leader, public vs. private funding). As the question and answer session came to a close, the moderator turned to us and asked, "All things considered, who has the better job?" And without a moment's hesitation, the chancellor said, "John does." After a few moments of stunned silence, the moderator exclaimed, "Why in the world would you prefer John's job? You're the leader of one of the largest and most prestigious research universities in the country, if not the world?" To which the chancellor replied, "True, but my ability to lead is largely constrained by the parameters and expectations of the position. Each day I follow a closely scripted and managed agenda that tells me where to go and what to do--and sometimes even what to say. Substantive strategic change happens slowly and gradually over long periods of time. John, on the other hand, gets up every morning at his 'small and unknown' college and says, 'Let's go here!'"

While I appreciated and understood the chancellor's sentiment, I felt obliged to inform the audience that even small organizations can still impose constraints on the work of the leader. Whether or not Jehoash aspired to be King, the position was running him, as opposed to the reverse. Aspiring to a leadership position is a noble thing, as long as you understand the responsibility it brings to *be* a leader, and not just have a leader's title.

- **Appearing clueless to the options that may lead to success**

    Elisha's death bed scene mirrors the opening narrative of his own leadership transition. In 2 Kings 2:12, we observed the apprentice Elisha exclaiming, "I see the chariots and charioteers of Israel!" Then, a flaming chariot whisked his mentor Elijah bodily to heaven. In this final episode of Elisha's life, King Jehoash makes the same exclamation. Since Elisha was not literally carried away by a flaming chariot, I can only speculate that the Elijah story was well known, and that the King was

Making the Iron Swim

keenly aware of the heavenly transition taking place in front of his eyes. In both cases, we see a series of events in rapid succession that initiates transfer of responsibility for them as leaders--and also presages their relative success as leaders in the future:

- **Despair:** A completely understandable reaction, especially if the mentor and the successor have enjoyed a long and intimate relationship. Even if a transition is planned and anticipated, the actual event can bring a sense of sadness, and a little panic for the new leader!
- **Desperation:** I call this the "losing the safety net" phase of leadership transition, where the leader officially hands over the reins of responsibility. It can also result in the "deer in the headlights" moment for the new leader. In the King's situation, it resulted in excessive weeping. Even for Elisha, there was a moment of fear and even questioning the existence of God when Elijah departed.
- **Direction:** The ultimate measure of success for transitions does not happen in the first two phases of despair and desperation. Those are normal, human reactions to a high stress, high risk environment. In fact, the honest expression of these emotions is a healthy thing, avoiding the mindless and dishonest bravado often expressed by new leaders who espouse a "No sweat, I've got this" attitude. Successful transitions result in independent steps of action that transcend the parameters within which the new leader has ever operated before. For Elisha, he parted a river,

> while the King defeated an overwhelming threat. For mentors, we should encourage our successors to make the role "theirs" as quickly as prudently possible. For new leaders, we should not feel overly concerned that our shift in style, approach, or direction will be seen as a criticism of our predecessor's leadership.

I was blessed to begin my first college presidency gradually, beginning as a senior leader reporting to the sitting president and then gradually assuming responsibilities over several months. This arrangement required a high level of transparency and trust, which we developed quickly and easily. Finally, the official transition day arrived. The outgoing president stood at my office door and said, "Good luck tomorrow." Of course, as a young, brash leader-to-be, I replied with an off-the-cuff response much too full of bravado. "Well, thanks, but I've already been doing the job for awhile. I don't expect too many surprises." The outgoing president smiled benevolently and said, "In theory, yes, but tomorrow my office will be empty. The sign of 'President' will be on your desk. There will be no one to bring your problems to for a solution or decision. Just wait. Buckle up. Good luck."

I think back on that exchange and still cringe. No amount of preparation or practice would ever compare to Day One in the big chair and the days that followed. The despair and desperation came in big waves, but eventually the position became more comfortable as I made decisions and led strategic directions. Whether good or bad, smart or dumb, I became a leader.

As it turns out, Jack was right. I could make the iron swim.

- **Turning every professional setback as a personal affront**

Over my 30+ year leadership journey, no single issue has appeared so quickly or dominated the collective debate on effective leaders like the focus on the leader as celebrity. With the advent of the internet and social media, the tendency of organizations to hire charismatic and attractive leaders has exploded to become the leader as organizational icon and media phenomenon.

With the focus on the celebrity of leadership, it's little wonder that leaders personalize their role, including the personalization of achievements and setbacks. Most leaders--and I count myself in this group--have become adept at using inclusive language, speaking of "we and us" and the value of "team." But, in reality, if we're painfully honest, we ultimately take the credit for every achievement and reap the lion's share of the financial and reputational rewards they bring.

We become adroit at justifying salaries, bonuses, benefits, and equity positions several multiples beyond the average employee. And why not? We're the smart ones. The ones carrying the organization on our shoulders. The ones casting the vision, setting the direction, inspiring the troops, facing the board, the investors, the media. Eventually, our true motivations emerge, revealing a level of personalization where the organization is an extension of ourselves.

As dangerous as that phenomenon may be for our personal lives as leaders, it pales in comparison to the consequences of personalization when things go wrong. When the failures and challenges loom. When plans fail, and they always fail at some point.

During these dark moments, the personalization of our leadership results in our taking offense at every bad outcome. The phrase "Why me?" comes to mind as we stumble from one piece of unwelcome news to another. And because we have become the public face of our organization, everyone sees the challenges facing the organization as our own personal failure.

In this last story of Elisha, King Jehoash comes weeping into the deathbed scene. Call me incredibly cynical, but I suspect that the King wasn't distraught over Elisha's impending demise because of any great love or personal connection he felt with the prophet. Nor do I think he's particularly upset because Elisha's passing would leave Israel without a direct word from the Lord. I believe the King was upset because he viewed Elisha as his personal source of superhuman power and strategic direction. Without Elisha, the King will be powerless and clueless--and he knows it. Now that would generate true despair!

Contrast this deathbed scene with the final paragraph concerning Elisha. After his death, Elisha continued to be on the hearts and minds of the Israelites, including which cave they buried his bones. In a supernatural event, coming into contact with Elisha's bones brought the dead to life. Speaking metaphorically, it raises the question of us as leaders--do we leave a trail of life-giving, life-enhancing memories and concepts to be remembered by our colleagues, or are we simply another face and name moving through the revolving door of our organization? Or worse still, do we leave a trail of destruction and damaged relationships in our wake?

The president of my undergraduate college would speak in chapel about the 23rd Psalm. Of course, anyone who grew up in Sunday School or attended church with any regularity could recite that chestnut. But, I found his interpretation of the phrase, "Surely goodness and mercy shall follow me all the days of my life" (verse 6a, KJV) to be particularly interesting. Rather than making the blessings of "goodness and mercy" something only we receive from God, he challenged us to be so in tune with God and His plan for our lives that we would leave a wake of goodness and mercy wherever we went. Sadly, that has not been true for my life and leadership as often as it should. But, our leadership role provides ongoing opportunities to leave those blessings in our wake, creating a legacy of leadership that transcends the personalization of our role into a collective commitment to goodness and mercy, and goodness and mercy, and goodness and mercy, through the years and across generations. We just have to start today.

So now I finish this study of leadership--of Elisha and Jack--by assuming Jack's role for you. Whether you're transitioning into your first significant leadership role, or you've been leading for decades, I know the difficulties and challenges you face and will face. I know the dark nights of despair and doubt and fear that will shake your very foundations. And I know the sense of powerlessness and cluelessness that will hound you during the most pressing moments of your leadership and the future of your organization. But I know you can handle the details, can make the critical decisions, can inspire and motivate your people.

I know you can make the iron swim.

Postscript

My wife, Gwen, and I returned to Nashville a few years ago to help my sister, Angie, care for my aging and ailing parents. In spite of the worries about leaving my career and starting in a new direction, I was excited to be back in the same community as Jack, and to rebuild our special relationship. As often happens in life, the demands of parental care dominated those early days, and time with Jack took a back seat for a future day.

Then Jack was gone. His passing was sudden and unexpected and full of the remorse that comes with broken promises and delayed plans. On the day of his funeral, I stood in the long line of people wanting to express the extraordinary relationship they enjoyed with Jack. You see, a great leader cultivates in many people the authentic feeling of being special and unique.

My time at the head of the line arrived, and I crossed to his casket, placed my hand on his and whispered, "I see the chariots and charioteers of Israel…."

About the Author

John Neal has been a musician, professor, university administrator, and business executive. He currently serves as a consultant and strategist on digital learning and lives in Nashville with his wife, Gwen. They are the parents of Abby, Grant, and Caroline, and the grandparents of Tatum, Clive and Rooney.

Made in the USA
Columbia, SC
27 April 2019